Dreams of a Mountain

DAN M. KHANNA

Copyright © 2015 Dan M. Khanna

All rights reserved.

ISBN: 0692384596
ISBN-13: 978-0692384596

DEDICATION

To my one and only lovely daughter, Pooja,
my best friend, my support, my security
Thank you most of all for believing in me.

CONTENTS

Prologue – The Dream

To My Daughter	1
The Defective Body	2
Artificial Dreams	3
The Story of My Life	5
A Perfect End	6
The Empty Shell	8
Happiness is an Illusion	9
Too Old for this Life	11
The Evil One	13
The Tormented Soul	15
In Search of Death	16
The Passerby	17
The Miracle of Life	18
A Child Without Hope	19
The Drinkers	21
A Beautiful Life	22
God and I	23
A Painful Process	25
The Emotional Rape	26
I am my Enemy	27
The Quandary of a Romantic	28
The Lonely Bed	30
An Unsettled Life	31
An Empty Vessel	32
The Ocean of Adventures	34
The Loser's Club	35
The End of Love	36
Life is an Erosion	37
Life is a Desert	38
Carved out of Existence	39
I am not the Same Person	41
I Have to Accept	42
If I Were Alive	45

The Sinking Boat	46
Chopping Life	47
I was Alive Once	49
A Touch of Class	50
The Final Obituary	51
What is Death?	52
Winding up Life	53
Crying is Fun	54
The Lonely Heart	55
Am I Worthy of Life?	56
The Final Interview	57
The Heartless Soul	59
If I had a Life	60
The Final Exit	61
The Future is Ending	62
I am not the Same Person	63
Staring at Fate	64
The Empty Bed	66
I am His Favorite	67
Protection or Punishment	68
The End of a Journey	69
Life After Death	70
The Blows of Life	71
To My Mother	72
The Quest for Love	75
The Divine Guidance	76
Let Past Go	77
Time to Move On	78
It is not the Same World	79
The Seeds	80
The Call of the Wild	81
Learning to be Alone	82
The Second Time Around	83
The Ancient	84

PROLOGUE – THE DREAM

I had a dream when I was growing up. Someday I will have a family and children. Maybe, we all think of such things. But, what was unique about this dream is that I wanted a daughter, just one daughter and no other child. Why? I don't know, but it felt right. I was lucky that I have my daughter. There is nothing more sacred and satisfying to nurture and love your child to see her blossom into a beautiful adult, loving, charming and smart, the perfect daughter anyone can have. Watching her grow inspired me to pursue my dreams of writing by believing in me and giving me emotional support and security.

What I wish is that she pursue her dreams, look up to the mountains and climb high to the skies and make a beautiful life for her and her family. This is still my dream.

Thank you, Pooja. Love, **Pops**.

Dan Khanna

TO MY DAUGHTER

I gaze at the sun
Caressing the ocean
Creating brilliant lights
And magnificent scenery
Then I think of you
My daughter
The nature's scene
Is so beautiful
But, you even more beautiful
Because you give joy
You give happiness
To lucky me
To have a daughter
That makes me whole
Without you
My life will be empty
You are the future
Carry it well
To the next generation
To start their life
With love and hope.

THE DEFECTIVE BODY

My body
Is a temple
Of illnesses
You name it
And they reside in me
Flourishing with enthusiasm
Cropping up in sequence
To warn me that they have me
They slowly eat me inside
While I fight their onslaught
One by one
They come to destroy me
To handicap me
One by one
I defeat them
And then face
Their next assault
But, my mind is strong
Body may suffer
But mind goes stronger
The battle ground
Mind versus body
In the end
The body will lose
But mind will triumph
For my thoughts
My knowledge
My emotions
Gave me a life
A life rich of living
And rich in faith.

ARTIFICIAL DREAMS

The dreams are there
Dreams of a great life
A perfect love
Success and fame
Respected by the world
And an end
That will make
The world miss you
Those are dreams
Artificial dreams
And they will remain just dreams
For the reality is
We struggle through most of life
We quest for love
Only to be disappointed and hurt
Existing on borrowed money
Mingling with few friends
Who are as lonely as you are
Sharing few laughs
And fleeting moments of joy
Living a life
Of proud existence
Doing the routine
But still dreaming
For dreams
Those propel you to the future
Lift your soul
With hope and aspirations
Float you

To a blissful state
Where the pain disappears
And life becomes a joy
The dreams.

THE STORY OF MY LIFE

The story of my life
Is simple
A very ordinary life
Some happiness
Some pain
Some love
Some rejection
Did love and lose
Made money
Lost money
Had relationships
Remain alone
It was
After all
Just a life
That will
Go unnoticed
What a life

A PERFECT END

When I was young
I would wonder
How my end will come
Will it be an accident?
Will it be natural?
Will I die of some disease?
Will I die a peaceful death?
Or, will I face a violent end?
Those were just the thoughts
That went through my mind
They didn't mean much
Just drifting melodies.

Now that I have lived
Most of my life
And the end draws closer
I reflect on my youth
And wish that
I died a peaceful natural death
But, that would not be possible
My body has taken a beating
From every illness and pain
Some nearly fatal
Some disabling me
As I live with the handicap
Of imperfect body
I reflect on
My imperfect life
And wonder

If this was all destined
An imperfect life
Coupled with an imperfect body
A match made in heaven
Creating a perfect end.

THE EMPTY SHELL

A shell
A covering
That shelters life
And protects the soul
As a sacred skin
That gives birth to life
'Til life
Is ready to
Burst out of the shell
And explore the universe
But then there are no shells
There is nothing to protect our shelter
There are just empty shells
Just scattered
In the world
To a life of non-existence
They remain alone
They remain empty
They are the abandoned ones
No one likes.

HAPPINESS IS AN ILLUSION

Happiness
Is not a four-letter word
But much sought word
Thinking
That if we are happy
We are okay
But happiness
Is an illusion
In the mind
Of the person
The poor person is happy
To last one more day
A sick person is happy
To feel better that day
A family man is happy
To sit with his family
But, then there is time
Time
The creator of happiness and sadness
No one knows
Where it stands
For time is an illusion
We are in it
And we are not in it
Time is universal
Moving our lives
In undulating curves
Creating a shroud of mystery
That tells us
When happiness happens
When it passes
We sit there

Flowing with time
Hoping it will stop
At the time of happiness
But it stays there
Just for a brief moment
And moves on
Leaving the impression of happiness
That should endure
Through time
An illusion of happiness.

TOO OLD FOR THIS LIFE

My life is young
But, I feel
Too old for this life
Why?
Is it the struggle for survival?
Trying to seek a better life
For yourself
And your family
When you realize
That life has passed you by
But, you still exist
Trying to carve a living
In an unforgiving world.

You feel one day
That after many years
You are still just there
Remembering the past
Trying to find
Morsels of decent memories
That propel us
Into the future
Clinging to past friendships
Stories of joy and gaiety
Hoping to live off the past
To the inevitable end
The mind is active
Searching for truth
But the body whispering
The game is over

You had a chance
You made some
You lost some
Now we are equal
Life is still young
But you are too old
Your time was
Your time is not now
You may be young
But old in body
For life moves forward
And nothing you can do
You are
Too old for this life.

THE EVIL ONE

She was evil
Quiet and cunning
Calculating and manipulative
Making Medusa
Look like an angel
Her demeanor deceived all
Her quietness concealed her unexplained past
Hiding cracks in her character
And using people
To build her wasted life
Portraying herself
As a victim of life and luck
Gaining sympathy from friends and strangers
To conceal her vindictiveness and callousness
Never laughing
Never exposing herself
Just in case
People may see
Her true colors
Hiding her past
In sympathetic colors
Treading life gently
Trampling and abandoning men
After she gets done with them
Extracting blood
To fulfill her survival instincts
She does anything to survive
With no scruples
Seeking prey after prey
'Til she sucks life out of them

Using her body
To gain victim by victim
Producing offspring
From any man
She can seduce
Using love as a lure
Just like a spider
Sucking life out
Of innocent victims
Like a black widow.

THE TORMENTED SOUL

The tormented soul
Searches for meaning
In unknown places
Trying to find
Answers that don't exist
It survives
Feeding off itself
As it slowly peels layers
To expose it
To find
An empty space.

IN SEARCH OF DEATH

I have lived
More than half my life
Now I wonder
What my second half will be
The first half was uneventful
Mostly struggle and survival
What will the next half be?
The same or different
What is gone may never come back
But the future comes tomorrow
I know it will wind up in death
The ultimate reward of living
I know it is there
Waiting and lurking
Asking me
When am I ready?
I was eager
Ready to embrace her
She cried with joy
At my affection and willingness
And embraced me lovingly
Caressed me with tenderness
And carried me gently
Into another world
That was much better
Than my present world
Peaceful and quiet
A world that I dreamed of
A world that is my final resting place
Before I start
My next journey
To my home.

THE PASSERBY

You sit on the corner
Of a street
And observe the people
That pass by you
Some you like
Some you don't
They are all unique
Yet so same
They carry the mistakes
Of being humans
They also carry the burden
Of being different
All going in the same direction
Trying to find
Something they never will find
They just walk
They just go
As I observe
The humankind
Just withering away
As a passerby.

THE MIRACLE OF LIFE

Life is a mirage
When you get there
It is not there
Just an empty illusion
That seems tempting
From the distance
We reach for it
But the distance remains the same
No matter how close you get
You are in life
But never with life
You are near
Yet far
Just like
A mirage.

A CHILD WITHOUT HOPE

A child without hope
Is a dead child
A child with hope
Is an unborn child
A child without opportunity
Is a lifeless child
Whose life died before birth
But that child is born
Somewhere every second
Without any hope of making it in the world
Without any future
It is a curse on mankind
That allows this to happen
Yet we live and ignore
What that child should do
We are incensed with our lives
Ignoring the future
Of innocent lives
Brought into this world
Through sex, lust or love
But not giving that spark
That propels and prepares
The child for the future
A future
In which the child
Creates a new world
Of love, hope and success
It is a disgrace
For humankind
To not let every child

Have an opportunity
To make a new world every child deserves
A better future
Than we had
It is a child with hope.

THE DRINKERS

Let's get drunk, my friends
For then we will share the truth
And for some moment
Share a fantasy life
And be close friends
Sharing jokes
Sadness and joy
Dreams of dreams
And forget
That a real world exists outside
For we are in a new world
A world of our own
That we know will not last
But it is our small world
That makes us
Tolerate the real world
A world
In which we just exist.

A BEAUTIFUL LIFE

Is life beautiful?
Yes, it is
Look around
See and feel the nature
The myriads of colors
The natural
Carving oceans and mountains
The running rivers
The innocent splendor of animals
The towering trees
The velour valleys
Yes, life is beautiful
And then we have
Humans
That defile a beautiful life
And destroy nature
In the name of progress
They kill their own earth
To survive and grow
And destroy
A beautiful life.

GOD AND I

If I had my way
I will tell God
And write a valid
Criticism of his creation
He is the best I am told
But the sad part is
That it is told by people
Who are not the best.

God, never liked me
Frankly, I never liked Him
Why should I?
As a matter of fact
Why should He?
He takes care of the chosen ones
And we pray
That sometimes later in life
We may become the chosen one
So after praying, kneeling, hoping, wishing
That someday
God will love us
But, God does answer
To whom, how, when, why?
I don't believe God is bad
It is just that
He is out of touch with us
He made earth
And let it go
Earth was just one of His sidekicks
One of fun and games
That He can watch on His computer
And entertain Himself

The follies of the humankind
Actually, God is not my favorite
But, I was afraid of Him
I know I could not fight Him
I was in awe of Someone
Who could come and strike me
When I did something wrong
Yes, I have been stuck many times
Sometimes gently
Sometimes hard
I cry out in pain
Then He holds me
Caresses me
And carries me
Life goes on
Between strikes and love
While I reflect on me and God
With no answers
And a strange relationship
That lasts forever
And that is the story
Of God and I.

A PAINFUL PROCESS

The memories
Of lost love
The feeling of
Warm embrace
The presence of closeness
The gentle sensation of touch
Now a distant past
But still very much present
As our emotions and body
Heals to erase the past
Which it never will
It is a painful process
Where tears wash the soul
Letting you drown
In memories
Of what was once
An everlasting love
Now, just a memory
That heals the heart
And move us forward
Wounded.

THE EMOTIONAL RAPE

The emotional rape
Is everlasting
It leaves a scar
That stays forever
Unhealed
And itching with pain
To remind us
That we are vulnerable
And our past remains with us
No matter how hard we want to forget
How we let time heal
We just get used to the scar
It becomes
Part of us
A body mark
Like a mole or a blemish
That we accept
As a beauty mark
A mark of life
That just made us.

I AM MY ENEMY

Most of us
Have some enemies
Some vocal, some silent
I may or may not have
I don't know
But, I do know
Who is my worst enemy?
It is me
I have no one to blame but me
For I had everything
A home, a life, a career
And then I destroyed everything
Through wrong decisions
Through wrong relationships
I was on top
Now, I am at the bottom
Staring at the top
I slid, I fell
I am my own enemy.

THE QUANDARY OF BEING A ROMANTIC

A person
Who can love
Can give himself to love
Willing to face
Any consequences
Is a rare species
That faces a quandary
If there is none to love
He holds the emotions
Wants to love
Wants to give
But there is no one to give
There is no one to love
He stands empty
Devoid of life
Searching the faces
Is that her?
Learning to live
With oneself
Bottling all emotions
Ready to shower any person
Willing to share love
The feeling of romance
That tingles, the sensations
Butterflies in the stomach
Hoping
That love will find a home
That can be called
A love nest
Harboring love and romance
Finding peace and contentment

A place, a person
To love, to hold
To touch, to caress
And feel the feeling of completeness
If it happens
It may not happen
That is the quandary
Of a romantic.

THE LONELY BED

The bed is empty
I lie on one side
Feeling the emptiness beside
I reach out
To feel the coldness of sheets
And wrap myself
In the warmth of emptiness
Lean over to feel a warm body
A body that gives me warmth
And gives me life
A touch, a feeling
But, it is empty
I long for warmth
The embrace of love
I grope about in the dark
Hoping my love will appear
But, then I wake up
Alone
In an empty bed.

AN UNSETTLED LIFE

An unsettled life
Is a street smart life
For it looks at life
Right in the face
 And asks?
What do you have for me?
What more can you give me?
I am not afraid of you
What can you do
That you haven't done
For a settled life is a boring life
Slowly eroding all passions of existence
An unsettled life is exciting
It gives you reason for living
To fight the challenges
Life throws at you
To become oneself
For life can never beat you
You are the master of life.

AM EMPTY VESSEL

An empty vessel
Stands alone
Waiting to be filled
By the elixir of life
The scent and sweetness
It can shelter in its bosom
And savor its flavors
As it gently
Caresses and kisses
The aroma
Enjoying the moment
For it knows
That elixir will not remain there forever
It will be snatched away
To give pleasure
To some other glasses
It will be empty again
But it is a vessel
It is there to hold
And pour to entertain and delight
It has only one purpose
To breathe life into the elixir
And intermingle with its contents
Learn and grow stronger
Taking pleasure
That it contained life
And then let it go
And wait for the next elixir
As it remains empty
Savoring the last memories
And awaiting the future

What gets poured in
It does not know
But it is a proud
Empty vessel.

THE OCEAN OF ADVENTURE

The ocean is vast and deep
I step in it
And I am soon
Engulfed in undulating waves
That toss me up and down
Sometimes throw me
Into the middle of ocean
And then pick me up
And throw me on the sandy beach
I gasp for breath
And then I am sucked into the water
Pulling me deep
'Til I am out of breath
And then
It lurches me
Into the open sky
'Til I am alive with fresh air
As I plunge back into the water
Holding my breath
Not knowing what impact awaits me
Will it be hard?
Will it be gentle?
Will I be held by gentle waves?
Or, thrashed with vigor and anger
I await my fate
And let it go
Let God decide
What it will be
For it is an ocean
An ocean of life
I am in it
And ready for adventure.

THE LOSER'S CLUB

There should be a place
A club
Where all losers in life
Can meet
And share their experiences
Of life and love
Shed a few tears
Share a few laughs
At the follies committed
And then move on to commit more follies
For there is nothing wrong about losing
For we did try
Not every effort results in a win
But, an effort is made
And that makes it all worthwhile
The losers club
Is a club of winners.

THE END OF LOVE

The end of love is never ending
For love never ends
It stays with you
'Til the day you die
For love is eternal
True love finds a place in your heart
Creates a nest
And nurtures its feelings
'Til it envelops the body and mind
It is in your blood
And feeds your soul
It is you
And no longer are you alone
For it will stay with you
'Til you die
You will die
But, it will continue
To a new life.

LIFE IS AN EROSION

A monument
That stands
On the edge of the sea
Is slowly ravaged
By the forces of nature
As waves slam into it
Eroding particles
That weakens the structure
As the wild sun
Bakes it into oblivion
As the wind
Shakes its foundations
Leaving the monument vulnerable
Just like life
As time erodes the structure
As living claws at its soul
As society molds it
Into a weakened structure
As relationships
Shake belief in humanity
Such is life.

LIFE IS A DESERT

As I gaze at the vast desert
In scorching sun
Seeing sand everywhere
Full of sandstorms and quick sands
The quietness is eerie
As if a sand blast
May come and strike you
You are thirsty
Seeking oasis of trees and water
The mirage driving us into an illusion
Of hope and faith
You reach for it
To find an empty land
We move forward
Only to step back
Searching for life
In a vast desert
Trying to find
An oasis of life.

CARVED OUT OF EXISTENCE

A sculptor
Stands before a marble slab
White, solid and rich
Imagining
What he can carve out of it
His dreams, his hopes
Can he give life
To this solid piece of stone
He picks the chisel
And strikes the first blow with the hammer
The pieces scatter
And he starts gentle erosion
As the stone begins to form
Into visionary images
The sculptor
With steady hand
Knows that one wrong stroke
Would kill the stone
And the image he is trying to create
Creation is a responsibility
For to breathe life into a stone
Is like giving life
To a dead stone
It is life
Waiting to come alive
As the sculptor chips
Eroding particles and pieces
As life chips away
Our heart and body
That is alive and beautiful

Just like the marble statue
That emerges from erosion
Of stone and soul
A master piece
A human.

I AM NOT THE SAME PERSON

As I stare at myself
In a shattered mirror
I see a person
That I do not recognize
I see a stranger
That is scarred by life
And eroded by luck
Whose dreams were destroyed
By wanton wanderings
And sealing hope
In dying monuments
It is a face
That once was innocent
Full of dreams
To leave a legacy of love and hope
But, now it stands among shattered ruins
Staring at a face
That is now carved and scratched
A face of a stranger
That was once me.

I HAVE TO ACCEPT

I have to accept
That I am alive against my wishes
I have to accept
That my dreams of childhood
Got scattered in the wind
As I stare at an empty wasteland

I have to accept
That my parents are not alive
To guide me and point me
In the right direction
As I flounder through life
Without their guidance and love

I have to accept
That I wasted my life
In frivolous pursuits
Of unreachable stars

I have to accept
That my health
Keeps knocking me down
While keeping me alive
As I await the inevitable

I have to accept
That I have no love in life
And I may remain loveless
Wanting love

I have to accept
That I live alone
In a desolate environment
Without friends or culture
Slowly withering away in life

I have to accept
That romance is just a dream
A wishful thinking
That once excited me
Now may remain dormant
Ready to explode anytime

I have to accept
That the end that I seek
May elude me against my wishes
And only come at its time
Not at my desire

I have to accept
That happiness is an illusion
That fleetingly touched me
And then vanished into thin air

I have to accept
That my life's journey will be alone
Searching for a place
That I would like to call home
But, I may never find it
And I may remain homeless
In my own home

I have to accept
My fate
My life
For it is God's will

And, I must accept
God's will.

IF I WERE ALIVE

If I were alive
I will question
The way I lived my life
Throwing away opportunities
Ignoring wise advice
Piling mistake after mistake
Running away from life
Squandering hopes
Making frivolous decisions on impulse
But then
I lived my life my way
Not a perfect life
But just an ordinary life
That will fade into a few remains
As I remember my life
If I were alive today.

THE SINKING BOAT

The sinking boat
Tries hard to stay afloat
As water seeps through its hull
Making it vulnerable
To the forces of nature
It discards its weights
To lighten itself
It reflects on
Its various journeys
Its ups and downs
As it awaits
Its final journey
To the bottom
Of the river
For eternal rest
In peace
In cool waters
Surrounded by the
Body of nature
It has found its home.

CHOPPING LIFE

The woodcutter
Looks at the tree
That stands inert
Full of leaves and strong branches
Ready to receive the blows without a fight
The woodcutter
Sizes the enemy
Picks the ax
And strikes a blow
The tree stiffens
A silent scream
As pain runs through the roots
Wondering
What it has done
It grew from a small seed
Provided shade to travelers
Provided fruits for the hungry
Provided flowers for beauty
But, today
It stands helpless
As blows strike it mercilessly
Its branches fall painfully
Soon it is stripped of all dignity
It stands bare
Without branches and flowers
As its trunk is cut
Exposing roots
'Til no life remains
To be hauled and burnt
For reasons
That it doesn't understand

But, its life is over
And it ceases to exist
As we humans
End our lives
Chopping trees.

I WAS ALIVE ONCE

I was alive once
Full of life
Ready to take on the world
Meeting challenges head on
Fighting for my spirit and soul
As life's onslaught
Wears you down
You are tired of fights
You don't give up
But, you accept
Not defeat
But the inevitable
We live
We are alive
'Til life subdues you
Into a bare existence
But, I must fight
I was alive once
I will be alive again
Full of life.

A TOUCH OF CLASS

A touch of class
Is a gift
That you are born with
It is not acquired
Or you learn in school
No book can teach you
Whether you have it
Or you don't have it
It becomes part of you
You exhibit class
In your actions
In your character
In your behavior
In your manners
In your attitude
How you dress
How you drink
How you deal with people
It becomes part of you
A second nature to you
You are class
You are a special class
Not just
A touch of class.

THE FINAL OBITUARY

We write our obituary
Many times in our lives
As we pass through
Different stages and episodes
We reflect on what we should have done
Instead of what we did
And then comes the final end
The last obituary
That is a history
Of all obituaries
For now there won't be any more
Life has ended
Only remains remain
A few words
In an insignificant paper that no one reads
It is a fitting finality.

WHAT IS DEATH?

What is death?
It is not the end of life
For life can end
Many times before death
People stop living
When they become
Pawns of the society
Existing for the sake of existence
Without laughter or passion
Each day is just another day
Going through routine
Just to kill the day
That is not life
Life without living
Is death of life
You have died
While living
And that is
Real death.

WINDING UP LIFE

There comes a time
In one's life
When you inventory
Your assets and liabilities
Take a stock of your life
And plan a winding up program
Discarding property
To lighten the load
Writing a will
To make it easy for heirs
Wishing what should happen
When you are gone
To simplify death
For now you are gone
But it still needs tidying up
'Til I fade away
And just remain a memory.

CRYING IS FUN

I cry often
As tears cleanse my face
With exploding emotions
I feel relief
As floods subside
Unburdening the soul
I can smile
At my wet face
For I am proud
I am human
I have emotions
I can feel pain and pleasure
And that is a gift of the Almighty
Crying is fun.

THE LONELY HEART

The heart
That pulsates on emotions
Is a lonely island
That wants inhabitants
Someone to reside in it
Someone it can love
And take care of
While it pursues the rhythm of life
Hoping to find peace
By giving love to a soul
But, it beats alone
In a constant rhythm
Swinging like a pendulum
Up and down
'Til it loses hope
'Til it realizes
Alone is enough
It must stop
The pendulum stops
Heart stops
Now, it is finally alone.

AM I WORTHY OF LIFE?

As I see the end of my future
I reflect on my living of the past
And wonder
Was I worthy of my life?
Did I live my life
As my parents wanted me to?
I don't know
But, I do know
That there is a nagging feeling
That something is not right
Whether I am not worthy of life
Or, life is not worthy of me
But, we are at odds
Me and my life
Yes, I made mistakes
Monuments of mistakes
And I deserve to be punished
But then events and episodes happened
Beyond my control
I don't deserve all the punishment
Delivered to me
So I remain at odds with life
Agreeing and disagreeing
But, am I worthy of life?
Yes, I think so
I did the best I could
Could have I done better?
Yes, but then
I was not worthy of life
The debate will go on
And last until eternity.

THE FINAL INTERVIEW

I stand at the gates
Ready to enter
But, I can't
I am asked to be interviewed by God
My final interview
To determine my ultimate fate.

In one sense it does not matter
For I am dead
But, it will still be nice to know
What God thinks about my life
Or, as a matter of fact
What I think about my life
How, did I perform?
Was I good or bad?
Was I a hit or a dud?
It will be nice to know.

The interview begins
I am told of all my mistakes
I am told of all my sins
Yes, there are some compliments
I don't feel that bad
For God did see a few good things in me
But, then I mumble excuses and situations
For then I did what I did
And justified my actions to feel good
But, I was wrong
I explain, I squirm
But God just stares
He knows it all

Why does He ask when He knows all?
His judgment is made
It is final
The interview is over.

THE HEARTLESS SOUL

There was once a soul
Full of adventure and love
It traveled through time
Living life to its full extent
And in the process got beaten up
Got hurt
Banged
For it was full of love
It had a heart
'Til it could bear it no more
For the heart got in the way of love
Its purity was too much for the society
Then one day
Soul let go of the heart to avoid future pain
And it became
A heartless soul.

IF I HAD A LIFE

If I had a life
I would ask it
Why me?
Why did you choose me?
To give me life
And then deprive me of happiness
Why would it give me birth?
Then make my life a struggle
Why would it find me mates?
That hurt and walk over me
It is not fair
But, no one said life is fair
It never has been
It never will be
So, I ask life
Can you be fair?
Life is quiet
There is no answer.

THE FINAL EXIT

We exit life
Many times in our lives
Seeking paths
That will lead us to the final exit
But, the final exit is final
It is the only exit that matters
For it is the end
The finality
When you don't have to worry about more exits
You have reached your destination
Whatever that maybe
Now you are free
At peace
And reflect on your journey
Was it good or bad?
Only God knows.

THE FUTURE IS ENDING

I see the future in the distance
And I see it falling off the cliff
What do I do?
Do I go near it
Or, step back?
I can always take a peak
Over the cliff
To see how far it is down
But, I am afraid to look
For I may not like what I see
I may get pushed over
Falling freely
To unknown spots
Or, just stand on the edge
Staring at the future
Prolonging the end
That must come
And stop the future from ending.

I AM NOT THE SAME PERSON

I look in the mirror
And see a face
That I don't recognize
I didn't know
I had become
A different person
Lines of life
Carved in my face
Telling a story
Of an ancient man
Weakened and beaten up
By the blows of fate
But still tall and erect
Proud and dignified
I am not the same
That's what the mirror says
But, I am the same person.

STARING AT FATE

As I stare at my fate
I wonder what it is thinking about me
I can't see it
But I know it is there
It has been an invisible force
That has guided me
Sometimes with love
Sometimes with hurt
I don't know why
I would like to ask it
What is my future?
But, then do I want to know it now?
For if it says
My future is bright
Should I stop all action?
If it says
There are problems in the future
Will that scare me?
Will I just stand still
And let fate pound me
Then, do I really have a fate?
Or, I create my own fate
With my own actions
Since, fate is invisible
I can ascribe any shape to it
Then I describe fate
In the image I perceive
Then fate is just a punching bag
For all good or evil in my life
Such is fate's destiny
Whether it creates my destiny
I don't know

But, I do know
It is there
For I am staring at it.

THE EMPTY BED

The night is warm and cool
I am asleep
But my mind is awake
The bed is large
Quiet and sober
As I stir to reach across the emptiness
To find a warm body
That I could touch
Embrace and hold
To sleep in peace
With the world in my arms
But all I do
Is touch an empty space
A cold and lonely space
That reminds me
That it is just an empty bed.

I AM HIS FAVORITE

I am His favorite
Of course, I am
Otherwise
Why will He take special time
To keep an eye on me
Somehow He has an unusual interest in me
He protects me
When I should be punished
He punishes me
When I should be protected
I get slaps
I get hugs
I get kissed on my forehead
I get spanked on my rear
Why all this attention on me?
Well, I am a perfect specimen
Of a regular human
Helpless, determined
And who needs guidance
I am an example to the rest of the world
I am His favorite.

PROTECTION OR PUNISHMENT

I know God loves me
But, I don't know
Whether His love is
My protection or my punishment
He protects me from my follies
Pulling me out of holes
That I dig for myself
Punishing me for the mistakes that I do
Hoping I will learn from them
So, I alternate
Between protection and punishment
His love and affection
For He is God
I am just a folly.

THE END OF A JOURNEY

The train stops
It is the last station
I have to get off
Pick up my baggage
Disembark
And search for an exit
It was a nice journey
Great sights, boring sights
Mountains and rivers
Plains and fields
All with their own beauty
But the journey is over
As I exit into a new city
I wonder what will I find
Should I find a resting place
And call it quits
Or should I search for a new adventure
In a new place
For the journey
Never ends.

LIFE AFTER DEATH

What happens to life after death?
Where does it go?
To heaven or hell?
Or, to another life?
That is a mystery
And will forever remain so
Is it something
To look forward to?
Or, will it scare me?
I know I have to face it
Will it ask for an account of my life?
Was I good or bad?
Did I do what I was supposed to do?
Will I be proud of my answers?
Or, will I be embarrassed by my answers?
Maybe both
I was not perfect
But neither did life treat me with kindness
I was just an ordinary person
Going through life
Awaiting the end
And taking chances with life
But, now that I am dead
Life is a past
I am there
Awaiting a judgment
And that is the life
After death.

THE BLOWS OF LIFE

I did get many blows
Some gentle, some painful
The blows to correct my path
Or to punish me
For my mistakes
With one purpose
To improve me
I don't know
I seem the same person
Waiting for the next blow
I know it will come
For I am human
Just an ordinary person
Living with blows.

TO MY MOTHER

Today is Mother's Day
I see sons and daughters
With their mothers
Happy and mushy
On this special day.

But, my mother
Is not with me
She is in the hands of God
Watching over me
With love and blessings
Always wishing the best for me.

I can feel her
Sense her presence
As if I were still a child
Held by her
Enjoying her nurturing
Finding peace in her arms
She is in my blood
She gave me life
And prepared me for this world.

Did I do justice
To her love?
I don't know
Was I a good son?
I don't know.

But I do know
That whatever I did or became
She would always love me

Selflessly and without expectations
All she wanted was
Good for me.

But, I know
I could have done more
Been with her more
I should have taken care of her
I did the best
But that is just an excuse
I had choices
I made the wrong choices.

But in all my follies
I thought of her every day
I wished for her guidance
I wanted to talk to her
Seek her wisdom
So I don't make mistakes
I was alone
I missed my mother
I miss her every day
To me, every day
Is Mother's Day
She gave me life
My soul
She is there
Blessing me
Loving me
Holding me
Wishing me the best
I know it
I do not need a special occasion

She is in me
A part of me
I miss her
Every day

THE QUEST FOR LOVE

Love
The famous four-letter word
That creates lives and destroys worlds
Is a powerful force
A source of energy
That I seek
Like a holy grail
For in it is salvation
The eternal flame
That consumes all of us
Life without love
Is a candle without flame
A body without life
It is a quest
That is destiny
For in its quest
I find delight
Pleasure and happiness
The ultimate salvation
The quest itself is a journey
A journey of life
Leading towards fulfillment
A journey that I will not deny myself
For the journey is me
It is love
For love and me are one
The quest is within me
It is there
Love is in the heart
Love is forever
It is divine.

THE DIVINE GUIDANCE

I have made so many mistakes
That now I seek
The Divine guidance
For my next decision
My record of mistakes is unbelievable
Volumes of work can be written on my mistakes
To serve as a lesson for future generations
For I never received divine guidance
I made my own mistakes
I am not proud of them
But, for the future
I do not trust myself
I need someone to guide me
Point me in the right direction
For there are not too many opportunities left
The road is ending
The journey must come to an end
But, there is a journey that still remains
I need a guide
So I don't stumble
I don't falter
I can't do it alone
My record is bad
I need guidance
A divine guidance.

LET PAST GO

The past is an anchor
That prevents you
From venturing into the future
To explore new worlds and experiences
Past is history
It was there
It is over
It served a purpose
It grew you
It made you
What you are today
But it is still past
Build on it
But do not dwell on it
It is a foundation
Of your experiences
It is over
The future awaits you
Let past go.

TIME TO MOVE ON

The time stands still
I am frozen in time
Suspended in mid-air
The past behind me
The future awaiting me
I am afraid to move
Will I blunder into the past
Or, get hurled into the future
To a destiny
That I don't know
To a place
That is unknown to me
But, I must move forward
For past maybe comfortable
But it is still a past
It is just memories
I cannot change it
No matter how hard I try
But, I don't try hard
For memories are precious
It is time to build on it
And create a future
That is full of good memories
The past is over
And the future is beautiful
It is time to move on
With vigor, with love
For future is life
And that's where we live
To make a world
That was in our dreams
It is time to move on.

IT IS NOT THE SAME WORLD

The world that I live in
Is not the same world
It has changed
Whether I have changed, or
Whether the world has changed
I don't know
Maybe, both changed
Did it change for good?
Did it get worse?
But, it did change
I don't see it in the same way
I don't see the innocence of honesty
The appreciation of trust
Selfness replaced by selfishness
Relationships based on advantages
Friendships temporary
Wisdom vanishing
Knowledge crippled
I know it is not the world
That I grew in
Now I am an alien
To a mediocre world
Tainted politicians and leaders
Greed worshipped
I don't know when that happened
But, it has happened
I see a world
Burning away in its own fire
Now it is consumed by it
It is not the world I know
Or, I want to know.

THE SEEDS

The seeds get planted
So that they can give life to flowers
That will blossom
And beautify the world
The seeds need nurturing
Water, soil and sun
Mixed in right proportion
To create a perfect environment for blossoming
And they bloom
The world is colorful
Everyone smiles and admires
And then someone
Plucks the flower
For a gift or to beautify their homes
But the flower is now ready to die
For its lifeline has been cut
It will last a few days
'Til it withers and dies
And then be thrown in the garbage
It has lived its life
And now must make way for new flowers
That still keeps sprouting from the seeds
The flower does die
It just gives life to new flowers.

THE CALL OF THE WILD

Someone is calling me
From the wilderness
Requesting my presence
In the dark world of life
Should I go?
The voice is haunting and seducing
I edge towards it
Tempted and scared
What will I find?
The lost dream
Or the blow of fate
But, it is a call
I can't ignore
My future awaits me
And I have to go
The call is for me
I must accept the consequences
Of the call from the wilderness.

LEARNING TO BE ALONE

It is not what I wanted
To be alone in my twilight years
But dreams are just dreams
As I learn to entertain myself
With music, food and arts
Sharing movies and theatre
With my soul
Cracking jokes
That make me laugh
It is not a bad life
Actually quite good
Full of love, security and warmth
It is my world
A quiet world
That I have created
I have learned to enjoy
A life alone.

THE SECOND TIME AROUND

Love is special
The second time around
As previous experiences
Have ground us
Into particles of hope
Grasping at love
That eludes us
Hoping that what we have lost
Can be gained
Clutching at straws
That may not hold us
As we fall
Into a deep abyss
Staring at the hole above
'Til it gets covered
By a wandering rock
That seals are fate.

THE ANCIENT

I look around me
And see people
Vanishing behind modern sculptures
Enveloped in electronic gadgets
That hide their true identities
I stand alone
Surrounded by crowds
That I don't recognize
Faces and shadows
That seem alien
I realize
I am ancient
A creature of the past
That believes in love
Honesty, integrity, values and decency
Words that mean
Nothing to today's crowds
Ancient words that once had meaning
Today they are buzzwords
That people throw out
To flaunt their ignorance
I am ancient
For friendships are genuine
Not based on selfish self-interests
Honesty meant
True to oneself
Not just a word
That has lost its luster
Integrity implied respect
Not creating new meaning
Based on the situation

Values meant beliefs and convictions
That one stood on
Not justification for any action
Right and wrong
The world has changed
And I have not
I am still from the past
That believed in something
Today the world is different
Hollow and shallow
An empty void
That has no spirit
It is a world
I don't want
I'd rather be ancient
Than participate
In a society
That exists
Just to exist
I am old
I understand
The world has passed me by
I am left standing
On the oasis of the past
Alone
An ancient.

ABOUT THE AUTHOR

Dan Khanna considers himself a traveler through life enjoying an adventurous journey. Dan was born in New Delhi, India. After he completed high school, at St. Columbus High School, Dan left India striking out for California via short stays in London, Montreal and Milwaukee, Wisconsin. Although his dream was to pursue a career in the arts, acting, music, and writing, a quirk of fate placed him in engineering college and pursuing a business management career, in which he excelled. Dan completed an undergraduate program in engineering, and a Master and Doctorate in Business Administration.

Dan worked in Silicon Valley's high technology firms and was a CEO and founder of several firms. He changed careers to be a professor. Now, he again is pursuing his dream in creative endeavors.

Dan is the quintessential Renaissance Man, whose interests span the gamut of the arts, sciences, history, social and political studies, classics and philosophy. His search for knowledge began in his early life where his father was the Chief Education Officer of Delhi and his mother was a Sanskrit scholar. Dan speaks English, Hindi, Urdu, Punjabi, and Gujarati.

As a child, Dan read voraciously, particularly enjoying novels, such as Sherlock Holmes, Agatha Christie, Earl Stanley Gardener, Ian Fleming's James Bond series and classic works of Shakespeare, Tolstoy, Dickens, Oscar Wilde, Thomas Hardy, and other writers. He was very interested in poetry and read English poems of Browning, Keats, Milton, Tennyson, and Frost, as well as, other poets, while mastering Urdu poetry. His intellectual interests including studying Western and Eastern philosophers, especially Socrates, from whom he learned questioning methodology employed in his research, lectures and seminars.

During his parochial education, Dan was interested in various sports: cricket, soccer and field hockey. His love for the arts and music was honed to a level that he performed in plays, movies and solo concerts.

Dan's present journey is devoted to creative arts and activities, primarily writing poetry, fiction and non-fiction books and plays, while continuing to acquire knowledge of diverse subjects. He has published one book and has written over twelve hundred poems. Dan has several non-fiction and fiction books in development.

www.ingramcontent.com/pod-product-compliance
Lightning Source LLC
Chambersburg PA
CBHW071313040426
42444CB00009B/2009